In The Event I Die

Instruction Manual and Information Guide
In The Event I Pass Away

Maisha Daniels

outskirts press

For requests or book orders email <u>a1financialconsult@gmail.com</u>

Disclaimer: The author in no way form or fashion considers the information contained in this book advice, legal advice, or professional advice. The information in this book is used for informational and educational purposes only.

It is encouraged to seek professional or legal advice.

This book does not replace a Will or necessary legal steps to set up assets in the correct manner indicated by each state in the event of death.

The intention of this book is to guide and give information to beneficiaries of the deceased in one place for needed information.

This Book Belongs To

____

Preface

This book is a guide that will help families during a very difficult time in managing the affairs of a deceased loved one.

The inspiration of this book was developed through a personal experience I went through myself when my paternal grandmother passed away. It was a very stressful and frustrating situation that I wouldn't want anyone to have to go through.

Having a Will is a must, but a lot of times even the Will doesn't have the bank accounts, passwords and all things needed to access that family members' information. No more having to wait for mail to come in to see what accounts your loved one had.

This book will outline designated beneficiaries, assets, and needful information so that families won't have to guess, fight or be lost during their time of bereavement.

I know we are in a digital world where almost everything is hooked to a device. While that is great; most devices, computers and laptops are password protected to keep people out. Having a physical copy of this book will allow the individual to hand this information over to their designated beneficiary, keep it in a safe place or even have multiple copies of this book to keep for themselves and distribute identical books to the intended parties.

My prayer is that this book adds value, organization and simplicity to you and your loved ones.

Sincerely,

Maisha Daniels

"A good man leaves an inheritance to his children's children"
-Proverbs 13:22 (NKJV)

Important Contacts

(Family member, Attorney, etc. Contact Information)

Beneficiaries

In the event of my death, here are the people/person
I have designated to inherit my possessions.

First & Last Name, Address, Date of Birth, Percentage

____

____

____

____

First & Last Name, Address, Date of Birth, Percentage

____

____

____

____

First & Last Name, Address, Date of Birth, Percentage

____

____

____

____

Beneficiaries

In the event of my death, here are the people/person
I have designated to inherit my possessions.

First & Last Name, Address, Date of Birth, Percentage

____

____

____

____

First & Last Name, Address, Date of Birth, Percentage

____

____

____

____

First & Last Name, Address, Date of Birth, Percentage

____

____

____

____

Contingent Beneficiaries

In the event of my death, here are the people/person I have
designated to inherit my possessions if the beneficiary dies

First & Last Name, Address, Date of Birth, Percentage

____

____

____

____

First & Last Name, Address, Date of Birth, Percentage

____

____

____

____

First & Last Name, Address, Date of Birth, Percentage

____

____

____

____

Contingent Beneficiaries

In the event of my death, here are the people/person I have designated to inherit my possessions if the beneficiary dies

First & Last Name, Address, Date of Birth, Percentage

____

____

____

____

First & Last Name, Address, Date of Birth, Percentage

____

____

____

____

First & Last Name, Address, Date of Birth, Percentage

____

____

____

____

Executor of Estate

Person or institution appointed to carry out terms of my will

Individual's Name or Institution, Address and Contact

____

____

____

____

Individual's Name or Institution, Address and Contact

____

____

____

____

The State of _____________________

County of

BEFORE ME, the undersigned authority, on this day personally appeared ________________________ known to me to be the person whose name is subscribed to the foregoing instrument and, being by me the first duly sworn, upon oath declared that the statements and capacity acted in are true and correct.

Signature____

Subscribed and sworn to before me this ____________ day of __________ 20____ A.D. to certify which witness.

Notary Public Signature _________________________________

Life Insurance Policy

Life insurance policy, Annuity, Long Term Care Information

Life Insurance Company, Policy Number and Contact Information

____

____

____

____

Life Insurance Company, Policy Number and Contact Information

____

____

____

____

Life Insurance Company, Policy Number and Contact Information

____

____

____

____

Life Insurance Company, Policy Number and Contact Information

____

____

____

Life Insurance Company, Policy Number and Contact Information

____

____

____

____

Life Insurance Company, Policy Number and Contact Information

____

____

____

____

Life Insurance Company, Policy Number and Contact Information

____

____

____

____

Commercial/Residential Properties, Land, ETC.

Commercial or Residential Properties I own as my
homestead and or rental properties or land owned

Property Address, Loan or Mortgage Information and Contact

____

____

____

____

Property Address, Loan or Mortgage Information and Contact

____

____

____

____

Property Address, Loan or Mortgage Information and Contact

____

____

____

____

Property Address, Loan or Mortgage Information and Contact

____

____

____

____

Property Address, Loan or Mortgage Information and Contact

____

____

____

____

Property Address, Loan or Mortgage Information and Contact

____

____

____

____

Property Address, Loan or Mortgage Information and Contact

____

____

____

____

Commercial/Residential Properties, Land, ETC.

Property Address, Loan or Mortgage Information and Contact

____

____

____

____

Property Address, Loan or Mortgage Information and Contact

____

____

____

____

Property Address, Loan or Mortgage Information and Contact

____

____

____

____

Property Address, Loan or Mortgage Information and Contact

____

____

____

____

Businesses & Trusts

Business/Trust owned, Partnered or Corporation

Business Name, Ownership Percentage, Affiliate Contact Info

____

____

____

____

Business Name, Ownership Percentage, Affiliate Contact Info

____

____

____

____

Business Name, Ownership Percentage, Affiliate Contact Info

____

____

____

____

Business Name, Ownership Percentage, Affiliate Contact Info

Business Name, Ownership Percentage, Affiliate Contact Info

Business Name, Ownership Percentage, Affiliate Contact Info

Business Name, Ownership Percentage, Affiliate Contact Info

Banks, Investments, Retirement Accounts

Bank accounts, Investment and Retirement/401k Accounts I own

Financial Institution, Account Number, Type of Account, Banker Info

____

____

____

____

Financial Institution, Account Number, Type of Account, Banker Info

____

____

____

____

Financial Institution, Account Number, Type of Account, Banker Info

____

____

____

____

Financial Institution, Account Number, Type of Account, Banker Info

____

____

____

Financial Institution, Account Number, Type of Account, Banker Info

____

____

____

Financial Institution, Account Number, Type of Account, Banker Info

____

____

____

Financial Institution, Account Number, Type of Account, Banker Info

____

____

____

Financial Institution, Account Number, Type of Account, Banker Info

---

Financial Institution, Account Number, Type of Account, Banker Info

---

Financial Institution, Account Number, Type of Account, Banker Info

---

Financial Institution, Account Number, Type of Account, Banker Info

---

Passwords, Pin Numbers, Safe Codes

Pin and Password Information for
Online Accounts, Apps, or Safes Etc.

Pin, Password, or Code for

____

____

____

____

Pin, Password, or Code for

____

____

____

____

Pin, Password, or Code for

____

____

____

____

Pin, Password, or Code for

____

____

____

____

Pin, Password, or Code for

____

____

____

____

Pin, Password, or Code for

____

____

____

____

Pin, Password, or Code for

____

____

____

____

Pin, Password, or Code for

____

____

____

____

Pin, Password, or Code for

____

____

____

____

Pin, Password, or Code for

____

____

____

____

Pin, Password, or Code for

____

____

____

____

Notes

Notes

A1 Financial Consulting LLC
A1financialconsult@gmail.com
www.a1finacialconsultingllc.com
972-515-9110

Facebook@a1financialconsulting

YouTube@a1financialconsulting

Instagram@a1financialconsulting